ABOUT THE FOODS YOU EAT
by Seymour Simon
illustrated by Dennis Kendrick

What is your favorite food? Do you like pizza and spaghetti? Or, would you rather eat hamburger and French fries? What about eggs—or a peanut-butter-and-jelly sandwich? Does it matter what foods you eat? Do you have to eat and drink at all?

Just think of something you really enjoy eating and let Seymour Simon help you find out about foods and you. He describes the way your stomach and other organs and parts of your body work to digest food so that it becomes part of your body. He gives information about the nutrients in food, good diets and bad diets, and the effects of different diets and foods on your weight, your energy, and general health. And he explains what is meant by a "balanced diet," and the basic four food groups which should be part of the food each person eats daily.

There are also a number of simple experiments, and clear illustrations throughout.

Also by Seymour Simon

ABOUT YOUR HEART
ABOUT YOUR LUNGS
DISCOVERING WHAT CRICKETS DO
DISCOVERING WHAT EARTHWORMS DO
DISCOVERING WHAT FROGS DO
DISCOVERING WHAT GERBILS DO
DISCOVERING WHAT GOLDFISH DO
DISCOVERING WHAT GARTER SNAKES DO
DISCOVERING WHAT PUPPIES DO
LIFE AND DEATH IN NATURE

LET'S-TRY-IT-OUT

ABOUT THE FOODS YOU EAT

by
Seymour Simon

illustrated by
Dennis Kendrick

McGRAW-HILL BOOK COMPANY

New York · St. Louis · San Francisco

For Jack, Vilma, Nicola, Jessica, Peter, and Ginsberg Farman

LIBRARY OF CONGRESS CATALOGING IN PUBLICATION DATA

Simon, Seymour.
   About the foods you eat.

   (Let's try it out)
   SUMMARY: Presents information about nutrients in food, good and bad diets, and the effects of different diets and foods on weight, energy, and general health. Also discusses how cooking affects the nutrients in foods.
   1. Nutrition—Juvenile literature. 2. Food—Juvenile literature. 3. Cookery—Juvenile literature. [1. Nutrition. 2. Food. 3. Cookery] I. Title.
QP141.S533   641.1   79–14395
ISBN 0–07–057457–X

Text copyright © 1979 by Seymour Simon. Illustrations copyright © 1979 by Dennis Kendrick. All Rights Reserved. Printed in the United States of America. No part of this publication may be reproduced, stored in a retrieval system, or transmitted, in any form or by any means, electronic, mechanical, photocopying, recording, or otherwise, without the prior written permission of the publisher.

123456789 RABP 7832109

Do you like to eat ice cream or pancakes?
Do you prefer hamburgers or eggs?
Do you like to eat raw fish or blubber?
What about rice or tacos?
People all over the world eat different foods.
You might like one food or another.
Yet no matter what you eat,
or what other people eat,
all your meals turn into you,
and all their meals turn into them.

You still look like you after a meal.
Your head doesn't look like a pizza pie.
Your arm doesn't look like a carrot stick.
Your foot doesn't look like a peanut-butter sandwich.
How do your favorite foods turn into you?
Why do you have to eat at all?
Does it matter what foods you eat?
Let's find out about foods and you.
What are you really made of?
Just as bricks are the building blocks of houses,
cells are the building blocks of living things.
Every living part of you is made up of cells.
Not only you, but all people, all animals,
and all plants
are made up of cells.
The cells in your body
come in many shapes and sizes,
depending upon the job they do.
You have millions and millions and millions of cells
in your body.
And each of your cells needs food.
Let's find out how each of your cells
gets the food it needs.

Think of a food that you really enjoy.
How about a slice of fresh-baked bread
or a sizzling steak?
Perhaps you would like a ripe apple
or a fresh strawberry?
Does your mouth water when you smell
something good cooking
and you think of eating?

Saliva is the watery substance that comes
into your mouth
when you feel hungry or begin to eat.
Saliva is a chemical juice that your body makes.
Suppose you have just taken a bite of some food
—pizza or carrots or
a peanut butter-and-jelly sandwich.
Your teeth cut and grind the food into small bits.
As you munch, saliva wets the food.
The food turns into a sort of moist glob.
It becomes soft and easy to swallow.

> **TRY THIS...**
>
> Chew an unsweetened cracker, such as a soda biscuit.
> Keep it in your mouth without swallowing for a few minutes.
> It will begin to taste sweet.
> The saliva in your mouth has started to change part of the biscuit
> into a sugar that your body can use.

Your tongue pushes the food around.
Finally your tongue pushes the food to the back of your mouth.

In the back of your mouth is an opening
to a long tube
that leads down to your stomach.
The tube is called the *esophagus.*
The esophagus is a special kind of muscular tube.
Food doesn't just fall down the esophagus.
The walls of the esophagus move in and out.
These movements push the food along,
like when you squeeze toothpaste out of a tube.
You don't have to stand or sit upright when you eat.
You can swallow food upside-down just as well as
you can right-side up.

TRY THIS...

You can prove this to yourself.
Lie down on a slant with your feet higher than
your head.
Take a bite of some food and chew it well.
Now swallow.
You will find that you can swallow
the food easily.
The food you swallow is pushed
into your stomach.
Otherwise the food would stick in your
esophagus.

Not all animals can swallow their food in the same way you do.
Dogs and cats can swallow with their heads down.
But chickens and other birds cannot.
They have to stick their heads up in the air
to let a beak full of food or water
slide down their throats.

When you've finished eating a big meal, you feel full.
You might feel like taking a rest.
But your body is still working.
It is busy changing your food into you.

TRY THIS...

Make a fist.
Place it just about where you think your stomach is.
If your fist is below your bellybutton, you are too far down.
Your stomach is higher than you may think.
It is just below your breastbone, on the left side of the body.

Your stomach is shaped like a narrow bag.
It has an opening at the top
and another at the bottom.
The openings have "drawstrings"
that open and close.
The drawstrings are really muscles.
When your stomach is empty, it is not much bigger
than a large sausage.
But when you eat a big meal, your stomach stretches
to hold everything from soup to dessert.
If you eat too much, your stomach swells up
until you can hardly take a deep breath.

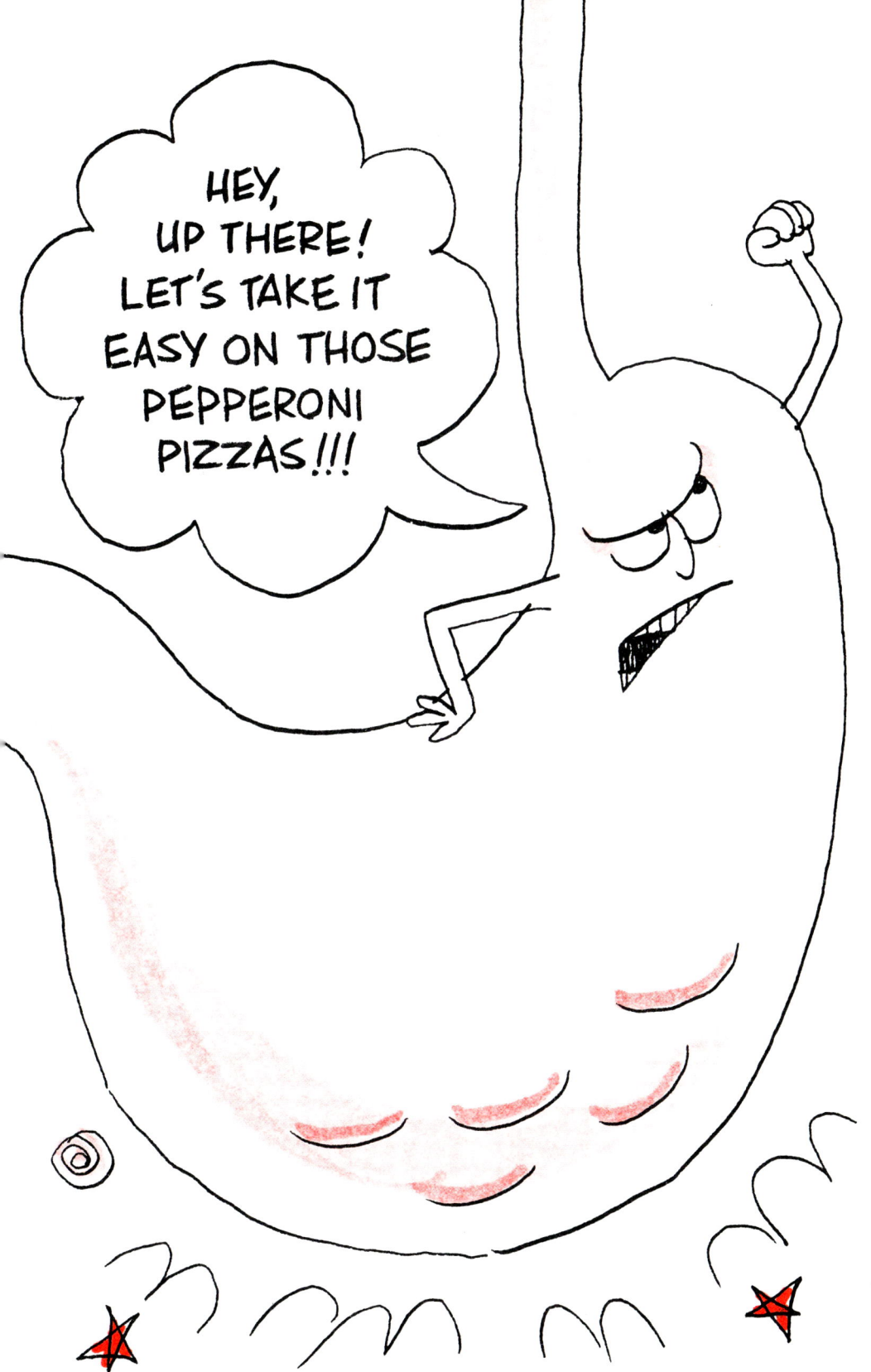

The food you swallow may stay in your stomach
as long as four hours after a meal.
Your stomach has rough and ripply walls.
The walls of your stomach churn the food around.
Your stomach also makes a liquid called *gastric juice*,
which contains some strong chemicals.
Gastric juice mixes with the food in your stomach.
It helps break down the food into very small pieces.
The food also becomes softer and more watery.
Here's how to see how churning motions
make the food more watery.

TRY THIS...

You will need two small baby-food jars
with covers,
two red cough drops, and water.
Fill each jar halfway with water.
Place a red cough drop in each of the jars.
Cover both jars.
Shake one jar up and down.
Let the other jar remain still.
Compare the color of water in the two jars.
In which jar did the cough drop become
watery more quickly?
You can see that churning food
in your stomach
helps to make the food watery.

Sometimes your stomach rumbles before a meal.
You feel hungry.
That's because your stomach muscles are beginning to squeeze.
Your stomach is also making gastric juice.
When food comes along, your stomach is ready to begin its work.
Your stomach is letting you know it's time to eat.

Even after staying in your stomach for several hours, most of the food is not quite ready to be used by your body.
More work has to be done to make the food ready.
The drawstring at the bottom of your stomach opens.
Your stomach muscles push the food
down through the opening a small amount at a time.

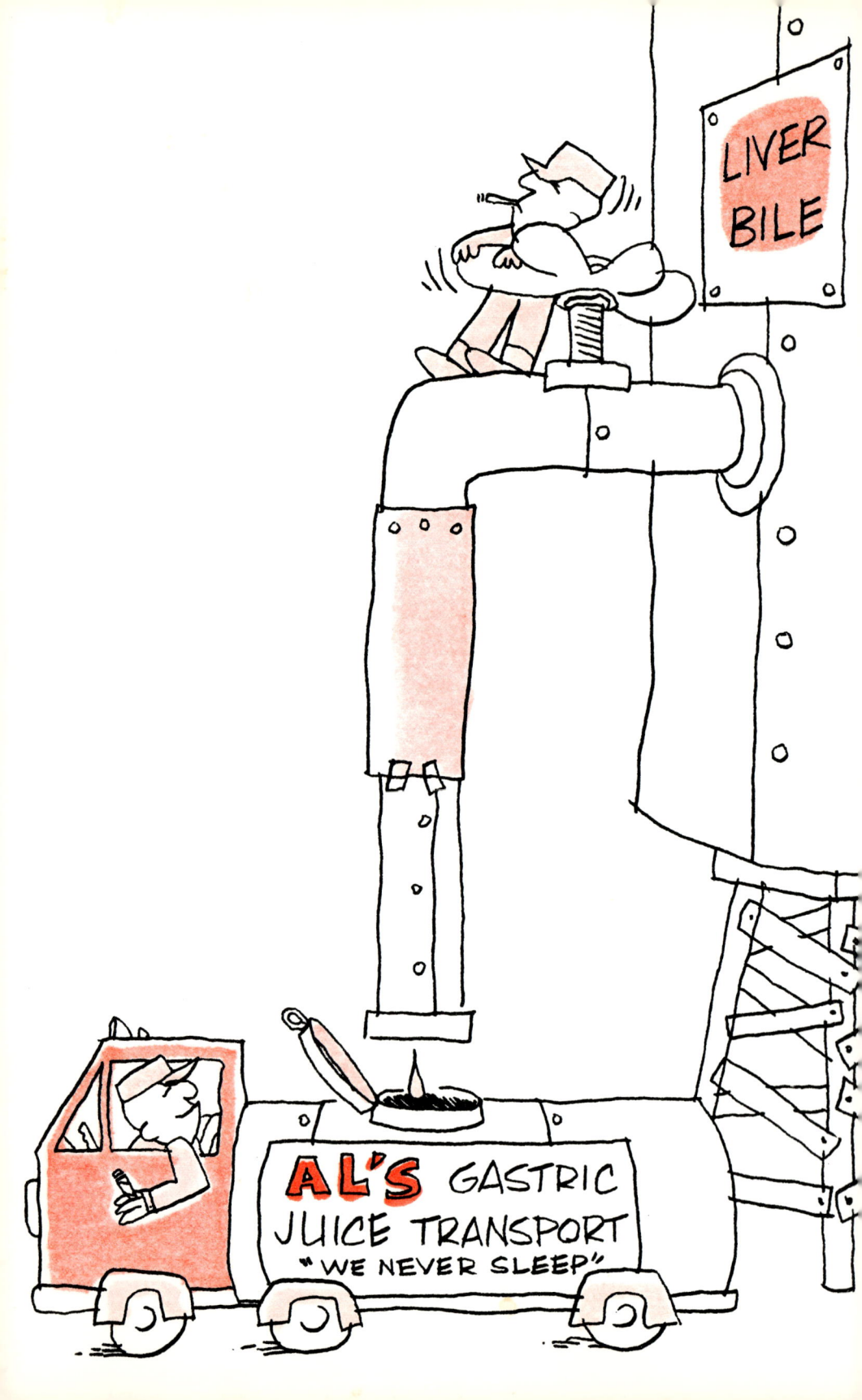

The opening leads to a long, narrow tube
under your stomach.
The tube is called the *small intestine.*
Chemical juices pour in onto the food
from all sides of the small intestine.
Some of the juices are made by
an organ in your body
called the *pancreas.*
These are called pancreatic juices.
Pancreatic juices help to break down foods
like cookies, vegetables, eggs, and meats.
Another chemical juice is called *bile.*
Bile is made by an organ in your body
called the *liver.*
Bile is a golden-brown chemical.
It is stored in another organ in your body called the
gall bladder.
Bile helps break down fatty foods
like butter and ice cream.
Still other juices come
right from the lining of
your small intestine.

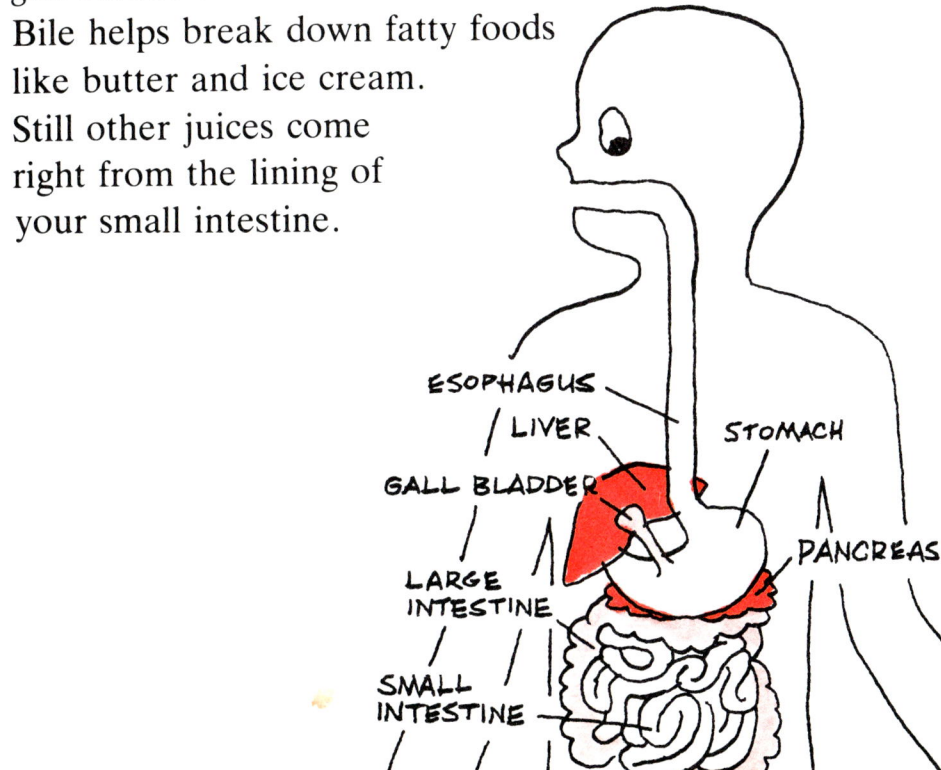

Your small intestine is four or five times as long as
your body.
But it is all coiled up inside the space
under your stomach.
Your small intestine has muscles like your stomach.
The muscles mash the food
and push it along the tube.
By the time food travels through your small intestine,
it has changed a great deal.
It looks like a kind of creamy liquid.
The food is now ready for your body to use.
We say that the food has been *digested*.
The parts of your body that work to break up food
are called the *digestive system*.

The digested food has to pass through the walls
of your small intestine so that it can get into the cells
of your body.
Here's how it happens.
Your small intestine is lined with tiny tubes
that wave back and forth.
There are thousands of them.
Each is finer than a hair on your head
and much shorter than the length of this line: -
The tubes are called *villi*.
The villi soak up digested food.

Here's how you can see how a watery substance passes through
the walls of some materials much like the villi.

> ### TRY THIS...
>
> You will need two cups, water, sugar, cocoa, a paper towel,
> and a teaspoon.
> Fill one cup halfway with water.
> Place a teaspoonful of sugar and
> a teaspoonful of cocoa
> in the water and stir it around.
> Fold the paper towel in half, and then fold it in half once again.
> Open it up so that it forms a sort of funnel with no hole in the bottom.
> Place the paper funnel in the empty cup.
> Slowly pour some of the mixture of water with sugar and cocoa into the funnel.
> Now taste the water that has filtered through the paper.
> It tastes sweet, but not like cocoa.
> The sugar passed through the paper, but not the cocoa.
> The cocoa pieces were too large to pass through the tiny openings
> in the paper.

The same sort of thing happens in your intestine.
Digested food can pass through your small intestine.
Food that is not digested does not pass through.
The digested food moves through the
thin walls of the villi
and into your bloodstream.
Your blood is like a supply train
that carries digested food.
Your blood travels all over your body
to each of your cells.
The pizza, carrots, and peanut butter you ate
are ready to turn into that very special person,
YOU!

Now let's see what happens to the undigested food
left in your small intestine.
It keeps moving along till it comes to a place
where the tube becomes much wider.
This place is called the *large intestine*.
It is much smaller but wider than the small intestine.
It has muscles like the small intestine.
But the large intestine has no villi.
Food is not digested here.
The end of your large intestine is called the *rectum*.
It is sort of a waiting room for the leftover part of
your food.
Your body gets rid of these food wastes
through an exit called the *anus*.
Altogether, a meal takes about one and one-half days
to travel through your body.

Now let's find out why you have to eat at all.
A part of the food you eat is used
by your body to grow.
Even when you are older and have stopped growing,
parts of you need to be healed and mended.
Each time you cut your finger or scrape your knee,
your body has to fix itself.
Every time you catch a cold or become ill,
your body has to protect itself.
You also use food for energy and for warmth.
You can see this if you use a thermometer.

TRY THIS...

Go outdoors on a cold day.
Check the thermometer
for the air temperature.
Now place the thermometer next to your skin
under your clothing.
Let it stay there for a few minutes,
before you read the temperature.
You can see that your body stays warm even
during cold days.

Your body stays warm because it burns food for heat and energy.
The burning is slow, and there are no flames or smoke.
But it is a real burning just the same.
You use energy all day and all night long,
even when you are asleep.
But you use more energy when you run or jump around.

You probably have heard the word "diet" when people talk about losing weight.

But diet also means all the foods you eat.
A *balanced diet* means that you eat enough,
but not too much,
of the right kinds of foods.
Just feeling full after you eat is not enough.
Let's find out what's in the foods we eat
so that you can see
just what is meant by a balanced diet.

The materials that your body needs from foods are called *nutrients*. Nutrients are grouped into five kinds: *proteins, carbohydrates, fats, vitamins,* and *minerals*.

Proteins are needed by your body for it to grow and become stronger.

Your muscles, skin, hair, and digestive juices are made mostly of proteins.

Foods that contain lots of protein are lean meats, chicken, fish, milk, eggs, nuts, and dried beans.

People your age need a lot of protein.

You should have some in your diet every day.

Carbohydrates include all sugars and starches.
Carbohydrates help supply your body with energy.
Your body needs energy to move, grow, repair itself,
and keep warm.
Carbohydrates are found in many kinds of foods.
Bread, cookies, spaghetti, breakfast cereals,
and soft drinks are high in sugars and starches.
Foods containing carbohydrates are usually cheaper
than foods containing protein.
They may also be more tempting to eat.
Some people eat too many carbohydrates,
and their bodies turn them into fat.
They may become overweight.
Overweight people may not be eating
a balanced diet.

DID YOU KNOW THAT ___ CONTAINS 440 CALORIES?

THERE'S A LITTLE PLACE IN MY NEIGHBORHOOD WHERE I CAN GET IT FOR 385!

Fats also supply your body with energy.
Dairy products and meats are good sources of fats.
You may think that you have more fats in your diet than you need.
Does this mean that you should cut out all meat and dairy products?

No, because a balanced diet can still include these foods.
But here's how you can cut down on the fats you eat.
Trim large pieces of fat off meat.
Eat fish or chicken sometimes instead of beef, pork, and lamb.
Keep down the amount of cheese, butter, and ice cream in your diet.

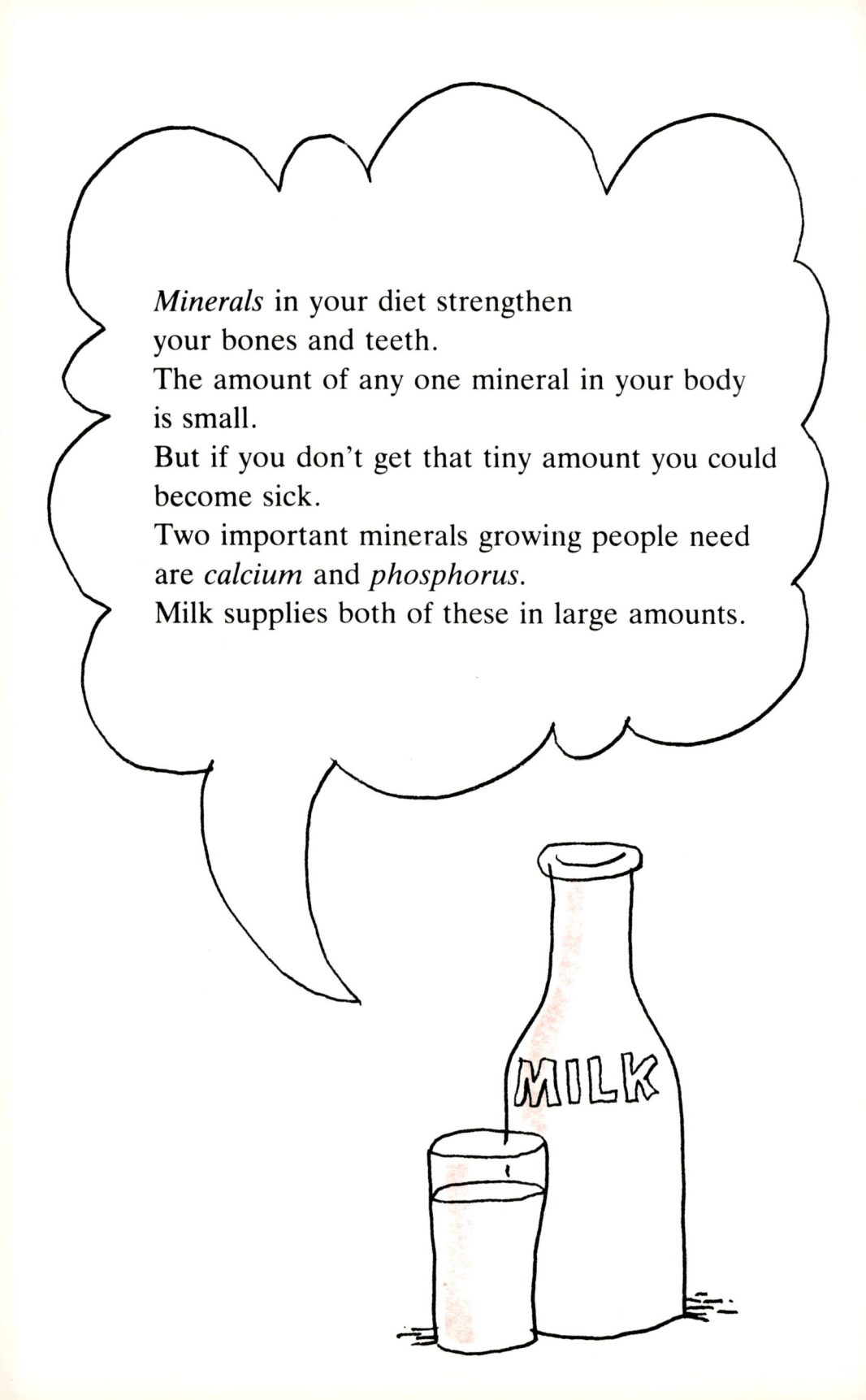

Minerals in your diet strengthen
your bones and teeth.
The amount of any one mineral in your body
is small.
But if you don't get that tiny amount you could
become sick.
Two important minerals growing people need
are *calcium* and *phosphorus*.
Milk supplies both of these in large amounts.

Another important mineral is *iron*.
Iron is needed for your blood.
Liver, lean meat, whole-grain cereals,
and enriched bread are good sources of iron.

PROTEINS
CARBOHYDRATES
FATS
MINERALS
VITAMINS

Vitamins are needed to keep your body working well.
You need only small amounts of vitamins.
If you eat enough protein, carbohydrates,
fats, and minerals
in your daily diet, then you are already getting the
vitamins you need.
Eating a balanced diet is the best way to get
enough vitamins.
You don't have to spend your money on vitamin pills
unless your doctor says you should.

Your diet also includes water.
Water is not a nutrient.
But about two-thirds of your body weight is water.
Nearly all foods contain some water.
Vegetables and fruits are mostly water.
Even meats contain a lot of water.
Milk, soup, and fruit juices give you water directly.

You need water all year 'round, every day.
But in hot weather, you perspire more.
Your body loses water.
You become thirsty when your body needs
more water.
So during hot weather you drink more to make up
for the loss of water.

Another important part of your daily diet is *roughage*.
Roughage is the part of fruits, vegetables, and grains that cannot be digested.
Even though it is indigestible, roughage helps to keep your stomach and intestines working.
Roughage passes through your digestive system and leaves your body as waste.

RUFF-age!

WOULD YOU BELIEVE MEOW-age?

BASED ON THE FORMULA THAT YOU NEED ABOUT 20 CALORIES PER DAY FOR EACH POUND YOU WEIGH... I CALCULATE THAT YOU SHOULD HAVE STOPPED EATING 2½ YEARS AGO...

You probably have heard people talk
about *Calories* in food.
A Calorie is not a nutrient.
When you count Calories, you are really measuring
the energy in food.
Almost all foods produce energy in your body cells.
Some foods contain more energy than others.
If you take in more food than you need,
the extra food is stored in your body as fat.
To grow and have enough energy,
you need about 20 Calories per day for each pound
you weigh.
For example, suppose you weigh 100 pounds.
Then you would need 2000 Calories every day
($20 \times 100 = 2000$).
The more active you are, the more Calories you need.
Unless you have a weight problem,
you probably don't need to count Calories.

THIS DONUT CONTAINS 130 CALORIES...

WHEN IT GETS TO 150 — SELL!

Here are lists of some foods that are either low or high in Calories:

Low-Calorie Foods
Fish, shrimp, and most seafoods
Poultry such as chicken and turkey
Skim milk, yogurt, unsweetened fruit juices
Eggs and many egg dishes
Oranges, grapefruit, lettuce, tomatoes, celery,
    and most watery vegetables and fruits

High-Calorie Foods

Steak, ham, pork, and prepared meats
such as hot dogs
Candy, cake, pie, ice cream, chocolate,
jam, and jelly
Soda and sweetened drinks
Bread, pancakes, waffles, and doughnuts
Peanuts and most other nuts
Potato chips, pretzels, crackers,
and other "snack" foods

Remember that a large portion of
a low Calorie food may
be the same in energy as a small portion of a high
Calorie food.
Suppose you wanted to cut down the number of
Calories in your diet.
Which would you eat for dessert—a piece of
chocolate pie or a piece of fresh fruit?
How can you choose a balanced diet from all the
different foods?

One way is to divide all foods
into four basic groups.
These are meats, milk products, fruits and
vegetables, and bread and cereals.
Your daily diet should include some food
from each of the groups.
You can make your own choices
within the food groups.
Each group includes many different foods.

Four Basic Food Groups

Meat Group: Meat, seafood, eggs, poultry, peanut butter, nuts, dried peas or beans. *Nutrients:* Mainly proteins, some fats, minerals, vitamins.

Milk Group: Milk, skim milk, cheeses, ice cream, yogurt. *Nutrients:* Mainly proteins and fats, some minerals and vitamins.

Fruits and Vegetables Group: All fruits and vegetables, fruit juices. *Nutrients:* Mainly roughage and vitamins, some minerals.

Bread and Cereals Group: Breads, cereals, spaghetti, noodles, crackers, cookies, cakes. *Nutrients:* Mainly carbohydrates and proteins, some minerals and vitamins.

Three meals a day is the custom in the United States and many other countries.
But it is not the only way to eat.

FO

Four or five smaller meals suit some people better. Eating smaller meals more often is one way to keep from overeating at dinner.

IF I ATE THAT, I COUDN'T LOOK MY MOUTH IN THE FACE!

Maybe you feel that you don't have much of a choice in choosing your foods.
You might eat lunch in a school cafeteria.
At home, everybody eats the same foods for dinner.
Where do your choices come in?
Perhaps you can choose what you want for breakfast.
Breakfast is an important meal.
You haven't eaten for twelve or more hours.
So skipping breakfast doesn't make sense.
You can feel tired and upset because your body needs food.
You can use what you have learned about foods to make breakfast an important meal for you.

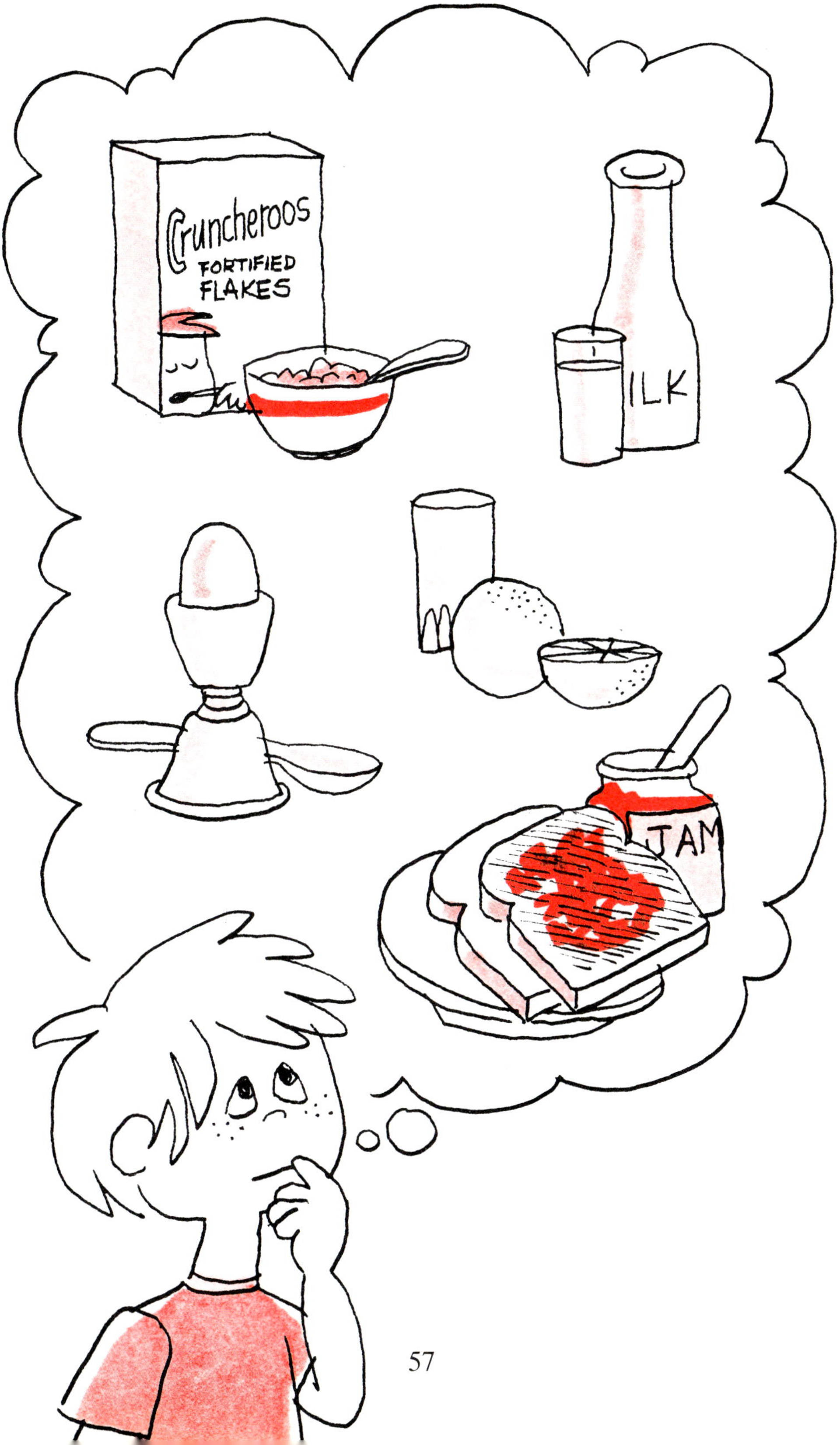
Cruncheroos
FORTIFIED
FLAKES
ILK
JAM

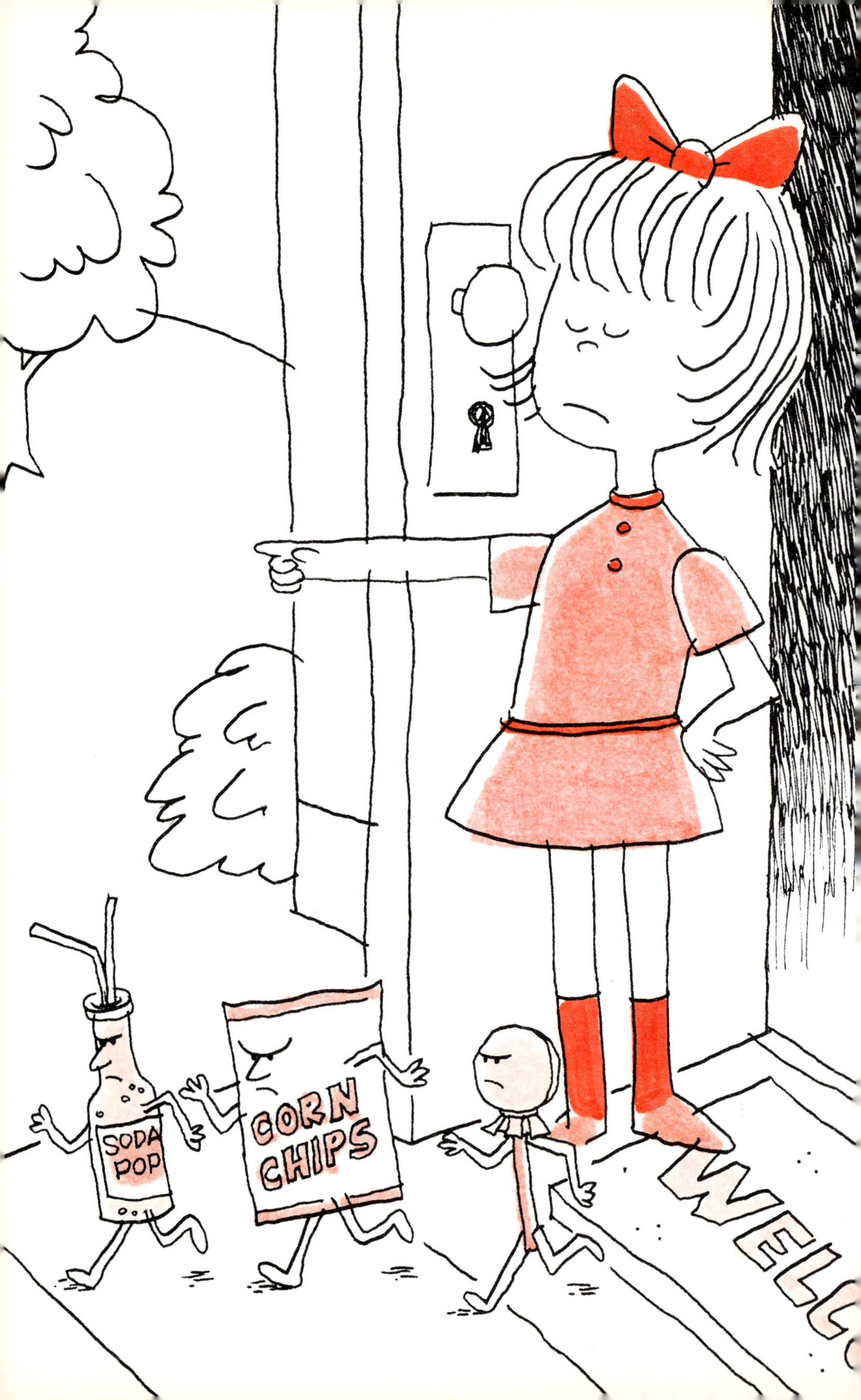
SODA POP
CORN CHIPS

Another choice that you have is what you *don't* eat.
It is easy to form a habit of snacking on "junk" foods
such as candy, cake, and soda.
These "junk" foods are high
in carbohydrates and fats.
They may give you more Calories than you need,
but they supply few proteins, minerals, and vitamins.
You can still snack if you choose other foods.
Eat an apple or another fruit instead of a
chocolate bar.
Drink a glass of fruit juice or milk instead of a soda.
Munch a stalk of celery instead of a cookie.

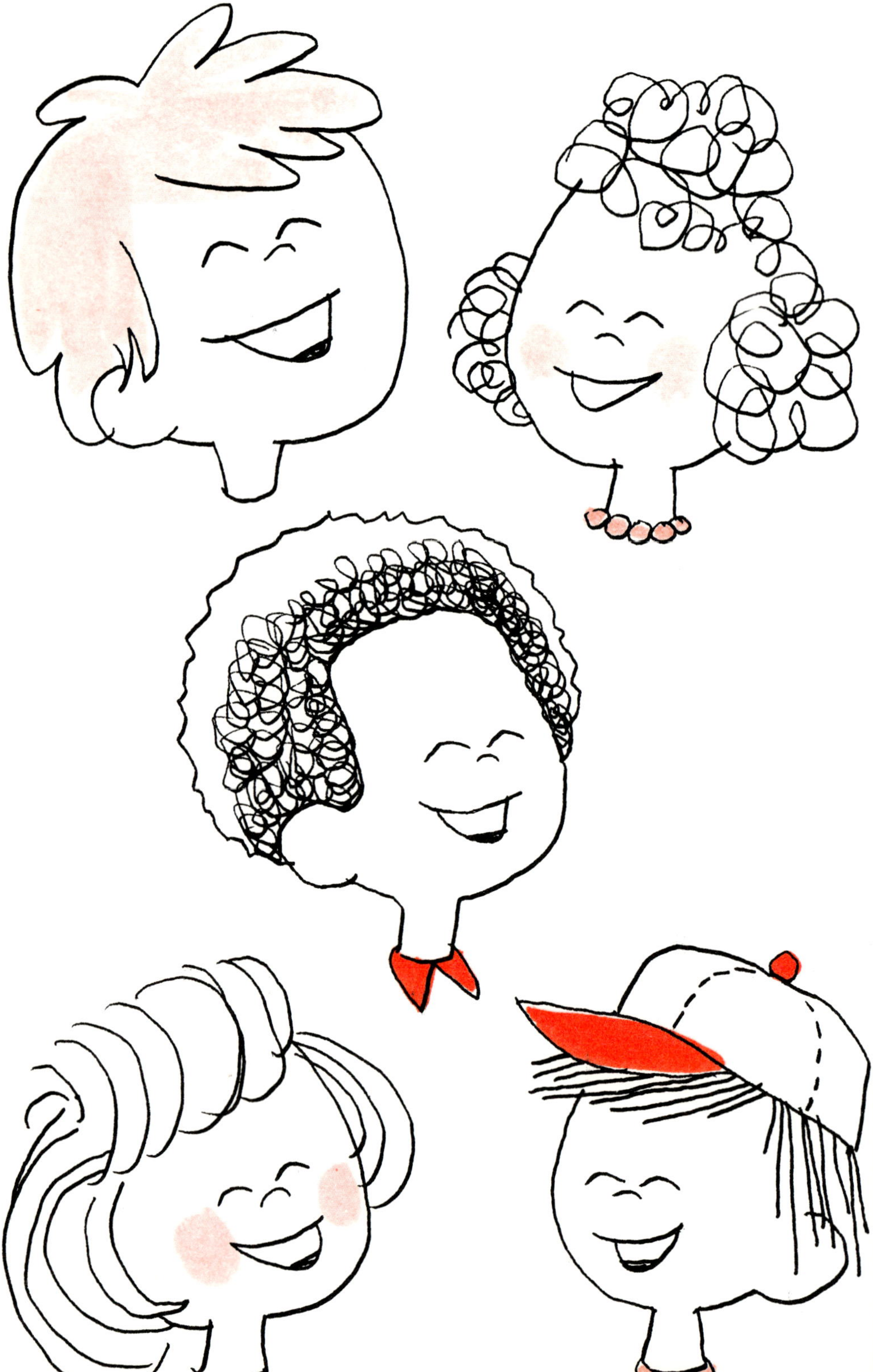

Ballplayers, tennis stars, dancers, athletes,
and workers of all kinds need to keep
in the very best shape.
You need to keep yourself in the best shape, too.
Eating the right kinds of foods is one way
to care for your body.
Getting the right amounts of rest and exercise
is another way of caring for your body.
The food and exercise habits you form now
will stay with you for a long time.

ABOUT THE AUTHOR

SEYMOUR SIMON is the author of dozens of science books, many of which have been chosen as outstanding science books for children by the Children's Book Council—National Science Teachers Association. These prize-winning books include ABOUT YOUR HEART and DISCOVERING WHAT PUPPIES DO, both published by McGraw-Hill. A teacher for many years, Mr. Simon is now devoting most of his time to writing and editing children's science books.

ABOUT THE ARTIST

Illustrator DENNIS KENDRICK received his training in commercial art at the Paier School of Art in New Haven, Connecticut. For the past ten years, he has taught painting to the handicapped at the Easter Seal Center in Bridgeport, Connecticut, in addition to freelancing as a graphic artist. At the moment, Mr. Kendrick and a partner are forming a greeting card company to publish their own designs. The artist has illustrated several children's books; ABOUT THE FOODS YOU EAT is his first for McGraw-Hill.

Mr. Kendrick lives in New York City.